An Insightful Journal for the Spiritual Journey

555

EXPERIENCE

©2020 by Roni Hopkins
All rights reserved.
ISBN: 978-1-7349035-2-2

JOURNALS OF REALIZATION

"The only truth one could ever die for is the truth they themselves have become"

Roni Hopkins is the creator of *Journals of Realization,* which are a collection of unique journals that specialize in spirituality and consciousness. She has traveled the world, connecting with all walks of life and lives her purpose dedicated to assisting others on their journey. The creation of these journals reflect those experiences and bring a level of universal insight to ones own spiritual path. Journals of Realization encourages you to discover and express your truth, wisdom and ever evolving awareness throughout the pages and beyond them through our virtual discussions.

Every path reveals its truth within you.

www.RoniHopkins.com

PREFACE

Human being or Being Human?
One is limited in nature and the other is eternity in time.
We find ourselves caught in between the two.

Before this life we are not human and after this life we are not any longer. It is only during the years of our lives can we have this Human experience.

To be placed in your body, your skin, with your family, your passions, desires, and strengths. To discover the perfect opportunity at the right place and the right time.

And with all the places you could ever be, you find yourself living on a specific coordinate of the earth that you call home

All of this

Every detail of your life amounts to your Human Experience.

It is filled with limitless moments that flow beautifully into the next. It is challenging, unknown and exhilarating as it contains so much for us to take in, in a seemingly short amount of time.

It is ALL here for us and our spirits take on the journey with survival and ambition from beginning to end.

Being Human is the experience of Life and we are all having 8 billion different experiences all at the same time.

Begin to embrace all that is in store for you.

Allow your tears to fall for joy and sadness
The heart to love from one person to the next
The motivation to finish one life chapter and the courage to start another

Every challenge, joy, passion and sorrow
Let it all be part of the experiences
The journey to discover what being human is for our souls.

This is your Spiritual Journey

From Pen to Paper

Your Thoughts

Your Experiences

Your Realizations

"*Life is the Experience of a Lifetime*"

Every aspect of our lives is compiled of experiences

Each moment

Each Second

That never repeats but allowing us an opportunity to expand, grow, and discover.

Being able to experience Life here on earth; is that not the foundation of all that comes thereafter.

Life is our spirit's journey to explore.

14

"The truest of all beliefs is only made true through experience."

One can know of the truth and even learn of the truth through others but knowing and actually experiencing are two completely different concepts.

The experience of a belief transforms your entire being to become the actual belief itself. So much so, the knowledge of the belief is no longer confined to it being a truth at all.

It expands beyond an intellectual validity into a living, breathing existence through you.

"Obstacles are the way to a path we have yet to tread"

Obstacles are what the mind creates when it cannot see a way out. As what we think are challenges are merely opportunities to approach life in a way we have not before.

Seeing all aspects of your life as an opportunity to grow, to change, to become the solution to problems that in hindsight were never problems at all.

It is a way to experience life constantly creating in and through you.

Life can be filled with endless opportunities to live, see, and experience it beyond what we perceive as a hinderance.

*L*ife is but a breath

What else do you have to give but of yourself. It is the only thing
You possess that has inexhaustible capabilities that can be given

This is the beginning of life

Life of altruistic ideas and efforts
To be a legacy of your own history

You can only be the best at nothing but yourself
You are the only one that is configured to do only which you can
Do

Can speak, can perceive, dissect, take it a part and what is left is
Nothing short of the best you can create

You cannot be mimicked or duplicated
As life continues to grow, you too grow with it

A form of you understood now is history to who you are today
And this is what Life does with us best

The most valuable thing you will ever discover is yourself
The true jewel that can shine like nothing else, can impact with
The force of a million prayers

Have the ability to influence everything and in time
Your worth appreciates through wisdom

Somewhere locked in conception and experience
You possess all that you are, all you ever needed to be and that is
worth breathing for

" When we are able to recognize Oneness in everything, then and only then, are we able to also recognize it in the fullness within ourselves."

A perfect mirror of reflected existence. This is the effective nature of consciousness. It unlocks the world to be a place of symmetry, a destination of imagination, a reality of dreams to explore.

The ability to connect spiritually in all that we see, feel, touch, taste and hear. It is in all that we encounter and all that life takes us through.

To recognize Oneness in Everything is to experience Eternity consistently unveiling itself without judgement of what it creates as perfection

58

"Time often gives the illusion of abundance and at the same time it gives us moments that we wish could last forever."

Take the time to be in the space, in the moment where you feel the seconds go by. Where appreciation settles in like the evening tide

Take each moment and allow lifetimes to be in them

When time shifts, we are obliged to flow with it, without consent On to another day, we have not experienced before

So in the present state, be completely immersed in all that is before you.

Let the oceans become your freedom

The sun become your life source

And nature become the purest of creation that you see

555

" You are the reason behind the why, The purpose of all that exist in your life."

Your life was created only for you to live. It is yours to cherish, to explore, to share, to challenge and to achieve. Whatever drives your desires to live it.

It is all here for you.

Though we often do not understand the why or the reason behind life happenings, we have to ask ourselves: Does life need to give us one?

The compilation of all of our experiences become the entirety of our life story and that is reason enough.

They are stories that become the conversations of our memories of life lived.

You being the purpose behind it all and realizing that every moment you experience, you are at the center of its creation.

555

" To know Oneness and to Live through the existence of the One itself is the destiny our souls desire for us to fulfill."

This is how we experience the omnipresent nature of our being. Seeing yourself and knowing yourself to be connected to every expression of life through every experience of life.

Whatever experience we find ourselves in, you experience the source of creation in it. It is beyond the emotions, past the judgements of the mind, the expectations and obligations that often lead to our own misperceptions.

The spirituality of our nature seeks only to connect with the source in everything. It brings the true purpose of oneness to the surface and there we find ourselves at peace.

*C*hosen

It comes to you from a place of familiarity so that you can accept
It as your own
You embrace forever in what could be forgotten

What could be timeless, the one thing that sends you soaring
As all things flourish in the seasonal rain and all things
Transform during the seasonal change

With the subtle hand of time moving you from situation to
Circumstance

Life is full of synchronicity and if you could cast a net into the
Oceans and pull at life's abundance
You wonder if your life would be the one you would have
Chosen

And you ponder

With wonders and what ifs
With anticipation and adoration
With one hand open and the other grasping to hold on

For the unknown is forever waiting for you

To understand life through a kaleidoscope of transience
Not to be consumed by it but seeing it through a full spectrum of
Imagination

Just so you can simply experience

And when the tides of life turn and on another eternal day
You may just find yourself casting your net
Hoping to choose another life well lived

> "The only way life can be fulfilled is by opening yourself to be filled by it."

The spiritual journey brings a level of vulnerability that many of us have never felt or experienced before. It is a state of such fragility and transformation of our most intimate, delicate parts of ourselves.

Those parts whether we are aware of them prior to this state or not, are the parts that unlock our true fulfillment here on earth.

It is All or Nothing.

True fulfillment is an All encompassing of the One within you and experiencing that oneness in its' entirety through every aspect of your life. It is a sustainable force that completes us, in and through our existence

As you awaken to spiritual consciousness, it will begin to fulfill you in the fullness of what eternity can offer.

> *"Traveling is transcending of the mind to unknown perceptions of new realities."*

This mindset prepares the stage for wherever you are in life. Whether you are going to foreign lands or open to seeing new possibilities in your day to day.

It keeps us exploring life from moment to moment.

The more we expand our parameters to experience the unknowns, the more we understand our connection to all of life. True empathy, compassion and oneness blossoms.

For all the experiences, far and wide, give our spirits permission to be free.

555

"It is more about the experience of life than the accomplishments of life themselves."

Your life is not going to live itself.

Do not dwell on how the chips may fall, what you may or may not possess in your present state or if your efforts will ever be noticed and validated

Just go for it.

The most powerful vantage point of putting action to any vision is watching how all the pieces divinely come together and experiencing the creation of your life right before your eyes.

In the end, you will undoubtedly live out all that is purposed and become a witness to something miraculous.

Something far greater, far beyond Life that flows within you and through you

www.ingramcontent.com/pod-product-compliance
Lightning Source LLC
Chambersburg PA
CBHW031116080526
44587CB00011B/1002